Cursive Handwriting

Practice Workbook for Teens

Children's Reading & Writing Education Books

BABY PROFESSOR

EDUCATION KIDS

Speedy Publishing LLC

40 E. Main St. #1156

Newark, DE 19711

www.speedypublishing.com

Copyright 2016

Practice
Cursive Writing

Trace and rewrite the following famous quotes.

Keep true to the dreams of
your youth.
—Friedrich Schiller

God couldn't be everywhere;
so he created mothers

—Jewish proverb

If you want to destroy

something then destroy your

negative thinking.

—Lopamudra N.

Be not afraid of going

slowly; be afraid only of

standing still.

— Chinese proverb

Success is the shadow of

hard work.

— Author Unknown

Learn from yesterday; live
for today; hope for tomorrow.
—Unknown Source

You must be the change you
wish to see in the world.
— Gandhi

I hear and I forget; I see
and I remember. I do and
I understand.
—Chinese proverb

There are no shortcuts to

any place worth going

— Helen Keller

In teaching others we teach ourselves.

—Proverb

Life is not about regrets,

but preparations.

—Tumisang R.

Happiness will never come to those who fail to appreciate what they already have.

—Unknown Source

All our dreams can come true
if we have the courage to
pursue them.
                    —Walt Disney

Without His love I can do
nothing; with His love there is
nothing I cannot do.
—Unknown Source

Nothing will ever be attempted

if all possible objections must

first be overcome.

—Samuel Johnson

There is only one happiness
in life —— to love and to be
loved.

—— George Sand

Cracks in the concrete serve as proof that even when you are strong you can fail.

— Neibor Mukwevho

One day your life will flash

before your eyes. Make sure its

worth watching.

— Unknown Source

I have learned to use the
word impossible with the
greatest caution.

—Werner Braun

Life is not a problem to be
solved, but a reality to be
experienced.

— Soren Kierkegaard

Books are like drugs the more
you read, the more you will
be addicted to reading.
—Lindelani M.

In three words I can sum
up everything I've learned
about life. It goes on.
—Robert Frost

Whether you think you can,
or think you can't, you're
probably right.

—Henry Ford

And in the end, it's not the
years in your life that count.
It's the life in your years.
— Abraham Lincoln

There is no elevator to
success. You have to take the
stairs.
—Author unknown

Where there is love there

is life.

—Mahatma Gandhi

Follow love and it will flee;
flee love and it will follow.
—Proverb

Friendship often ends in love
but love in friendship, never.
—Charles Caleb Cotton

Choose a job you love, and
you will never have to work
a day in your life.
—Confucius

Love is a serious mental

disease.

—Plato

Words are easy, like the wind

Faithful friends are hard to

find.

—William Shakespeare

The one who loves least
controls the relationship.
— Unknown Source

Love is an act of endless
forgiveness; a tender look
which becomes a habit.
—Peter Ustinov

Life can only be understood backwards; but it must be lived forward.

— Soren Kirkegaard

Friendship often ends in love

but love in friendship, never.

—Charles Caleb Colton

You must be the change you

wish to see in the world.

----- Mahatma Gandhi